Health AND Fitness

Staying Healthy

A. R. Schaefer

Heinemann Library,
Chicago, IL

www.heinemannraintree.com
Visit our website to find out more information about Heinemann-Raintree books.

To order:
☎ Phone 888-454-2279
💻 Visit www.heinemannraintree.com to browse our catalog and order online.

Edited by Rebecca Rissman and Catherine Veitch
Designed by Kimberly R. Miracle and Betsy Wernert
Picture research by Elizabeth Alexander
Originated by Dot Gradations Ltd.
Printed in China by South China Printing Company Ltd.

14 13 12 11 10 09
10 9 8 7 6 5 4 3 2 1

Library of Congress Cataloging-in-Publication Data
Schaefer, Adam.
  Staying healthy / Adam Schaefer.
    p. cm. -- (Health and fitness)
  Includes bibliographical references and index.
  ISBN 978-1-4329-2769-1 (hc) -- ISBN 978-1-4329-2774-5 (pb)
  1. Health--Juvenile literature. 2. Hygiene--Juvenile literature. 3. Excercise--Juvenile literature. I. Title.
  RA777.S34 2008
  613--dc22
                          2008052298

Acknowledgments

We would like to thank the following for permission to reproduce photographs: Alamy pp. **4** (© Jupiter Images/Polka Dot), **5** (© Image Source Black), **7** (© Dennis MacDonald), **8** (© CW Images), **16** (© Picture Partners), **22** (© Interfoto Pressebildagentur); Corbis pp. **17** (© Fancy/Veer), **27** (© Randy Faris); Getty Images p. **25** (Charlie Schuck/UpperCut Images); Photolibrary pp. **6** (Inti St. Clair/Blend Images), **10** (Stockbyte), **11** (Creatas/Comstock), **12** (Liane Cary/Age Fotostock), **13** (Banana Stock), **14** (ER Productions Ltd./Blend Images), **15** (Uwe Umstätter/Mauritius), **18** (Tomas Rodriguez/Fancy), **19** (Corbis), **23**, **24** (Asia Images Group), **26** (Banana Stock), **28** (Blend Images), **29** (Andreas Schlegel/fStop); Shutterstock pp. **9** (© Zeljko Santrac), **20** (© MaszaS), **21** (© Estelle).

Cover photograph of a boy brushing his teeth reproduced with permission of Photolibrary (ER Productions Ltd./Blend Images).

The publishers would like to thank Yael Biederman for her assistance in the preparation of this book.

Every effort has been made to contact copyright holders of any material reproduced in this book. Any omissions will be rectified in subsequent printings if notice is given to the publisher.

Contents

Staying Healthy 4

Exercise and Good Food. 6

Keeping Clean 8

Washing Hands 10

Staying Clean. 12

Tooth Care. 14

Being Careful About Germs 16

Getting Hurt. 18

Wearing the Right Clothes 20

Being Careful Outdoors. 22

Keeping Your Mind Healthy 24

Getting Enough Sleep 26

Getting Started on a Healthy Life . . .28

Glossary 30

Find Out More 31

Index. 32

Some words are shown in bold, **like this**. You can find out what they mean by looking in the glossary.

Staying Healthy

Healthy people feel good. They have plenty of **energy** to work and play. You can stay healthy by taking good care of yourself.

Healthy people can enjoy time with their friends.

It is a good idea to start healthy **habits** now. It will be easy for you to get used to healthy habits now, and then you will have them for life.

Visit your doctor and dentist regularly for checkups.

Exercise and Good Food

Eating well is a big part of a healthy life. Try to eat a lot of foods that are good for your body, like **fresh** fruits and vegetables. Try to only eat a few sweets and **fats**.

Fresh fruit is full of many **vitamins** to keep you healthy.

Swimming is a good way to exercise.

Exercise is an important part of a **balanced**, healthy life. Being active will keep you in good shape.

Keeping Clean

Cleaning your body washes away germs and dirt.

Good **hygiene** is an important part of a healthy life. It is important to keep yourself, your toys, and your clothes clean. You can keep your body clean if you take a bath or shower every day.

It is important to keep your hair clean. You should wash it often and get regular haircuts. You can also have an adult check your hair regularly for head lice.

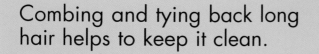

Combing and tying back long hair helps to keep it clean.

Washing Hands

Your Choice:

You have been playing outside all morning. You are hungry and it is time for lunch. Should you wash your hands or just wipe them off?

Our hands carry germs, even if we cannot see them.

You should always wash your hands before eating. It is important to wash them with soap and water to remove any **germs** that could make you ill. You should also keep your fingernails short and clean.

Wash your fingernails to get all the dirt out.

Staying Clean

Keep your sheets and blankets clean.

It is healthy to sleep in a clean bed. Eating food in bed is a bad idea because crumbs can get in the sheets.

Have an adult help you keep
your clothes and bed clean.

Clean clothes are important too. Clean clothes
help keep away **germs** and insects. Wearing
clean clothes helps your skin stay healthy.

Tooth Care

Your Choice:

You know how to brush your teeth twice a day. One morning while brushing, your tooth hurts. Should you tell an adult or just wait for it to feel better?

Brush your teeth at least twice each day.

Your dentist will help you keep your teeth and mouth healthy.

Tell an adult if your tooth hurts. Maybe you need to go to the dentist. The dentist will check your teeth and gums.

Being Careful About Germs

You cannot see **germs**, but they can make you sick. Germs are **bacteria** and **viruses** that can get into our bodies. You might get sick if there are too many germs in your body.

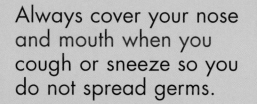

Always cover your nose and mouth when you cough or sneeze so you do not spread germs.

Germs are spread from person to person when we cough or sneeze. Sometimes germs are carried by animals. You can wash your hands with soap to kill most germs.

Always wash your hands after playing with a pet.

Getting Hurt

Your Choice:

One day you get cut on the playground. It is a little cut, but it is bleeding. Should you just wash it off and forget it, or should you tell someone?

Adults can help when you are sick or hurt.

It is important to tell an adult when you are **injured**. It is also important to tell adults when you do not feel well. Sometimes we all have to go to the doctor.

Nurses and doctors can help us feel better.

Wearing the Right Clothes

The weather changes at different times of the year. It can be very hot, very cold, or rainy. It is important to wear clothes that **protect** your skin and body.

Warm clothing protects your body from cold weather.

Wear a hat in hot weather to protect your head and keep you cool.

When it is very hot, wear cool clothes and a hat. When it is rainy, take a raincoat or umbrella. When it is cold outside, make sure you have on enough clothes to stay warm, especially gloves and a hat.

Being Careful Outdoors

Your Choice:

You are walking in the park near a tree. You see a nest with a lot of insects flying around it. Should you take a closer look or stay away?

Some insects make large nests or hives.

It may be interesting to take a close look, but bees and wasps can hurt you. It is important to tell an adult where the nest is right away. You should always watch where you play and make sure the area around you is safe.

Never pick up broken glass or trash.

Keeping Your Mind Healthy

Reading a book is a good way to take a break.

Good **mental health** is as important as keeping your body physically healthy. Mental health means the health of the mind. This means how you think and feel.

One way to have good mental health is to make sure you get plenty of rest and have fun. You should do many different activities and spend time with your friends and family.

Gardening is one way to relax.

Getting Enough Sleep

Your Choice:

It is bedtime, but you do not feel tired. Can you stay up really late as long as you do not feel tired?

Sometimes you might want to stay up late and watch television.

Getting enough sleep is important for everyone. You should try to get at least ten hours of sleep each night.

Sleeping rests your body and gives you energy.

Getting Started on a Healthy Life

Get started with healthy **habits** today. The sooner you begin, the better you will feel. Good habits can last a whole lifetime.

When you are healthy, it is easier to be happy.

Adults do the same things as you to stay healthy. Healthy habits are important for a long and happy life.

Adults should also try to stay healthy.

Glossary

bacteria tiny creatures that live in air, water, animals, and plants. Some bacteria can make people and animals sick.

balanced life that includes different exercise and healthy eating

energy power needed for your body to work and stay alive

fat oil found in some foods

fresh fruit and vegetables that have just been picked. They are not cooked.

germ tiny creature that can cause illness

habit thing you do often

hygiene keeping yourself and your things clean

injury when you or another person gets hurt

mental health health of the mind. How you think and feel.

protect when something protects you it keeps something bad from you

virus tiny organism or life form that makes people sick

vitamin thing found in some foods that helps the body to grow and stay healthy

Find Out More

Books to Read

Duckworth, Katie. *Health*. North Mankato, Minn.: Smart Apple Media, 2005.

Knowlton, Marylee. *Safety at School (Staying Safe)*. New York: Crabtree, 2008.

Royston, Angela. *Get Some Rest! (Look After Yourself)*. Chicago: Heinemann Library, 2004.

Royston, Angela. *Staying Healthy (My Amazing Body)*. Chicago: Raintree, 2005.

Royston, Angela. *Why Do We Need To Be Active? (Stay Healthy!)*. Chicago: Heinemann Library, 2005.

Websites

http://kidshealth.org/kid/
This website has lots of information on how to stay healthy, as well as games, quizzes, and experiments.

Index

adults 9, 13, 14, 15, 18,
    19, 23, 29

bacteria 16, 30
bathing and showering 8
bed, clean 12
bees and wasps 22, 23

checkups 5, 15
clothes 20–21
    clean clothes 13
    cool clothes 21
    warm clothes 20, 21
coughing and sneezing 16,
    17
cuts 18

dentists 5, 15
doctors and nurses 5, 19

eating well 6
energy 4, 27
exercise 7

fingernails 11
friends 4
fruits and vegetables 6

gardening 25
germs 8, 10, 11, 13,
    16–17

hair washing 9
hand washing 10–11, 17
hats 21
head lice 9
healthy habits 5, 28–29
hygiene 8–9

injuries 19
insects 22–23

mental health 24–25

pets, playing with 17

reading 24
relaxing 25

safety 23
sleep 26–27

teeth and gums 14–15
teeth, brushing 14

viruses 16
vitamins 6

washing 8–11, 17

001427326

E
613
SCH

Schaefer, A. R.
(Adam Richard)

Staying healthy